Altar

poems by

George Eklund

Finishing Line Press
Georgetown, Kentucky

Altar

for Laura

Copyright © 2019 by George Eklund
ISBN 978-1-64662-038-8 First Edition
All rights reserved under International and Pan-American Copyright Conventions.
No part of this book may be reproduced in any manner whatsoever without written permission from the publisher, except in the case of brief quotations embodied in critical articles and reviews.

ACKNOWLEDGMENTS

I would like to thank the editors of the following journals in which these poems first appeared:

The Heartland Review--------------"A Cup of Tea," "The Strange Document,"
Referential Magazine---------------"Rhodes," "White Hands"
Priestess & Hierophant-------------"Frontier"
The Wax Paper---------------------- "Altar" "Madonna"
Descant---------------------------- "An Orchestra"
Poetry Fix-------------------------"Escape from January"
The Lindenwood Review-----------"Waterbody"
Gravel------------------------------"The Lamentation," "Sonata by the Sea"

Publisher: Leah Maines
Editor: Christen Kincaid
Cover Art: Laura Eklund
Author Photo: Laura Eklund
Cover Design: Elizabeth Maines McCleavy

Printed in the USA on acid-free paper.
Order online: www.finishinglinepress.com
also available on amazon.com

Author inquiries and mail orders:
Finishing Line Press
P. O. Box 1626
Georgetown, Kentucky 40324
U. S. A.

Table of Contents

An Orchestra 1
White Hands 2
Cantata San Jose 3
Blue Snow 4
Sonata by the Sea 5
Answer to the Tree 6
The Lamentation 7
On a Quiet Night in Iceland 8
A Cup of Tea 9
The Strange Document 10
The Bracelet 11
The Red Bird 12
Rhodes 13
Madonna 14
The Surprise 15
Altar 16
Frontier 17
Before a Confession 18
Essay on a Blue Field 19
The Request 20
The Way to You 21
A Word 22
The Uniform 23
Water Body 24
Escape from January 25
The Last Reader on the Beach 26
The Aztec 27
The Gaze 28
O Small Towns of Ohio 29
Requiem 30
Now That We Are Still Thieves 31
The Shrine 32
Essay in Late Summer 33
The White Lawn Chairs 34

An Orchestra

An orchestra needs two conductors
And eight French horns,
The wind in its wild self
Breathing and disappearing
With its cousin, the light,
Abstract as a thought.

The windy dark maims us
In the night window
Up the arms
To the eye flesh.

What are my elements,
The figures I cannot touch?
A literate mark
Asks for everything.

What are the elements beyond prayer,
Beyond my idiocy and memory of fish?

The mind creates itself
At the edges of things
We cannot hold,

The elements loaded upon
Those burning vehicles
Driven by blue violinists.

White Hands

How beautiful the distant doors
And your white hands
Upon my imaginary face,
Your breathing through the gauze of a flower.
The changing colors of a wall.

In the tangled fumes of the dusk
You can see the ricks of your girlhood.
It is so quiet at the edge of the flesh
An ocean of light receding
Into a thought,
The lights of freighters
Consumed at the horizon.

How lovely the lost script,
The seizure of the dew in its rebirth.
Our bodies lighten
Beneath the mask of the moon
And the universe awakens
At the tips of the fruit tree
On the lip of the storm,
Star to tiny star in the mind
Where no mother can reach.

Cantata San Jose

I am still walking in the chemical rain,
The chemical dark of the thigh muscle
Where the cramp hatches itself
Into a blossom that fills the space
Of our death.
One might stand on a corner in the west village and freeze
Hoping to become a serious particle
Beneath the unreal peaks of lightning...

Prepare to lose power
Prepare to have your name passed
Over the net or flung
Into the soup bowl
Prepare for the lights to go out
At the edge of your San Jose
And your dear remorse swallowed
In the sounds of the vacant coast.

Blue Snow

I have been named
With a dark stick
Moving in the dirt
In the shadow of the flame

When the blue snow comes at dusk
I pour red wine into the cold
That holds the sharp edges of the trees

And boys walking home
Dragging their shovels in the faded air
Ready now for darkening

The blue snow held in the scent of the bay
And the white hulls pulled up to the shore

I comb my beard
And speak another language
To the new snow that fills

My mother and father
And the dreams we will never know
Of each other

We look in our mirrors
As if no one could see us.

Sonata by the Sea

The one-armed man kept fanning himself,
The woman in white lifted her baby from the sand.
Only one horse could be seen on the beach
As a thousand eyes dwelled on the waves.

The woman in white gazed at the one-armed man,
The one-armed man closed his eyes
And mounted the wild horse.
A thousand sinners considered the sun.

The baby wept in the salty heat
And the wild horse stepped to the lip of the wave.
A thousand lovers touched the scars on their bodies
And the blind man felt himself lifted from the sand.

Answer to the Tree

In public interviews
Some days my fingers seem smaller,
On other days, they seem to lengthen
Toward the waves of trees I once knew.

We answer the tree or run to safety
Chased by the animals of silence.
Time cannot be lost.
"It's so dark in there," said the old woman
Drinking at the edge of the woods.
What would she take with her.

A white butterfly lands upon her face.
It has been created many times,
An answer for the tree
Although there are no questions
In its roots or leaves.

The Lamentation

Water drops hit the porch,
While my beard grows
I have no plan
Except to keep thinking
At the edge of the rising planet.
It is wild to come upon it
Unnamed in the acids of my mouth,
A molecule moving seizure to seizure.

I rise from the bed,
I touch her beautiful foot
As I walk by
I send a prayer of four words
That no one will hear.

Sweet beer, thank God for my coma,
My resurrection.
Without a plan, I am dragged
By my hair and throat to the sea,
My beard growing
At the edge of the rising planet.

On a Quiet Night in Iceland

On a quiet night in Iceland
He imagined a gentle climb
To the origin of bells

But the mind remained in its punishments
Breathing hour to hour
In the body's helplessness,

Forever the vulnerable bones of the child.
The moths still attached to his shoulders
An outdated man could no longer

Curse the world without harming himself.
A little morning blood
Stained the whiskers and the pillow

But he had managed to protect the stomach
With a pill, rising from trench to trench
In search of the mother of bells.

In its green northern glow, the night
Nearly killed him in his silence.
He welcomed the journey of sleep's preparation

And attacked himself with broken wings,
His violence held in a whisper
And spooled upon itself.

A Cup of Tea

He would sip his lukewarm tea
And imagine wooden sailing ships
Loaded with bags of sugar,
Boxes of limes carried north

What could tear him apart
Now that much had been given away,
Starting with the wooden cradle
And the weeping cherry tree.

The thing he composed would stay open
And incomplete, a broken tooth
Numbed in the mouth
Waiting for the face to finish its war.

He would finish his sunny cup of tea
And mumble at the edge of the soup
While jets assembled in his dream
Above the hills of Pakistan.

A window would flash upon the window of his screen,
The words were many
And the songs were all drinking tunes
As all music is for drinking

And the tomb just now visible
At the edge of the sea.

The Strange Document

The grass is coming,
My stomach tries to heal.
In town, they are filling the new jail.
The warmth comes, I am created
In the strum of the ukulele.
The clouds broke so easily
As with the purpled mind.
Mother has been put away again.

I wrote a note to the earth
Hoping to surrender to the moths,
That they might lift me
From the river that died
Before it could be held.

The grass is good upon my face
As I hide from the wind
And the rusted strophes.
What a strange document
I am making today
With a hand that loses circulation,
A foot that is a memory

The head held out of time
Beneath the shadow of the hawk
And a death that comes from the stars.

The Bracelet

I wait in the empty house of the prayer,
The thieves now less than a mile away.
Soon the cold, soon the name and the falling leaves.
Oh, the gray whiskers and the stray notion,
The waters of the unknown
Splashed upon my face.
What isle of numbers fills the forehead,
What if a god took over the mind,
A mouth closing upon the blossom.
Warm rain at dawn, a memory of the last beer.
Strange nature, the flags flap lazily
In opposing directions above the lodge.
From terrible indecencies
Silence explains the wind
In a world without remedy,
We know a star as a chemical in the stomach.

Touch me in the empty house of the prayer.
Three figures made of shadow and cloaked in rags
Have come carrying every question ever asked.
How far is the sea?
How shall we eat?
Where is the new book, my dear, the one you hold
To your breast as the wind howls
Out of the mirror.
Touch me at the edge of two storms,
My chemicals are changing and the world must follow,
Holding itself again and again
So we may not bring harm.
To the thieves I offer the bracelet
I made for my mother, created
From string and small colored tiles
And golden beads that were real.

The Red Bird

The red bird streaked across Troy's lawn,
A drop of blood sweat whisked from a face.
The natural world waited for nothing.
A man in a crooked beard and spotted hands
Drove the ridge homeward
Speaking into the air around his head.

If the mind is forgiven
The hands will make their pledge.
And the red bird shall reign
In its semaphore.
We push away from the table
Having forced ourselves to love a country.
The apocalypse is happening
So slowly, most are able
To ignore it.

Rhodes

On the island of Rhodes I knew so little
Down the sunlit walks above the bay,
On the beach we played chess
With the priests of 1972,
Then took the final cab ride to Lindos,
A perfect place for making love and dying.

When my brother appeared in my dream
I began to know more
Of what we carried to the windmills at night.
Every thought became the beginning
Of a miracle—

Lifting a small block of wood
From the tide of a warm sea,
The gulls swooping in their hungers,
The robust Germans crying *Wolfgang, Wolfgang*
Frolicking in the surf.

Now I am nearly old in Lindos.
In the left hand a golden glass of warmth,
And in the right, a lengthening rope
That sinks beneath the starry waves
And my brother watching
In the breeze that strikes the windmill blades.

Madonna

The Madonna carried in a rickshaw
Her hair braided this time
The bright threads of her thoughts
Severed but soon to lengthen
In the silicon of the sunset,
In the maze of flowers
The seizure of the wind gust.
Yearning for the dewberry and the footstep,
The opening of all time
The brick in the smoke of itself
She fills a necessary uselessness.
Maybe she will change her name
To Agatha or Sophie.
She is coloring with my daughter
An outline of the massacre in yellow
Wiping out the gallery and the grove.
Maybe she will spill her purse
Upon the ragged cobblestone
And smile as children cluster
At the humming insurrection.

The Surprise

I am always surprised
When she desires me
Surprised by our bodies
As if earth were remade
Dreamed again
In the thick veins of our hands
In the new core of the nova
The rags of space
The identity of the clay
The fabric of the silence
Held mouth to mouth
In the dark space
Between the branches and leaves.

Altar

One makes little altars repeatedly

I drop my weight into a chair
At the desk
Amazed by the violins and their particles
And the quiet color of my clothes

Every picture that comes to me
Is a derangement
Place from place

A pellucid cry across the barren Easter
The pointless stroll through the city

The wheels of grief complete
And our hands follow our eyes
Skimming upon the circles of the altars.

Frontier

Wet sky, wet life
In the language of the cumulus
The constant breakage of the sky

The circumference of my will
Is small
The wet sails of the light
In my hair

Our long drive connects the elements
The spasm is something holy
Holding us as we cannot hold it
In a bay or a yellow room

Every place may be the strangest place in the world

The child is pulled from the ditch
The cloud pulled from the air

The virus is a terrain
Fastening itself to what breathes.

Before a Confession

A wind comes to rearrange the face
What can a thought do?
In the function of a tree's leaves
Or an ocean wave…
The beach walkers believe they are not lost.

From a distant mind the trains arrive
Filled with sleepy commuters
Who recognize me at the shore
Where children have been robbed of their signatures.

Old women squint on sandy trails to the sea
They have all killed a monster
With their brain cells
And now stare eastward into their lives

With the pocked vitamins halved in his coat
A man goes driving
Toward a station by the sea
With a bottle of wine
Beneath an avalanche of clouds,

The voice of water
Deflects the thinking of the world.

We arrive, remade in our chemicals
Looking for impossible form, our legs
So we may not fall
Before a confession,

Speaking other languages
When we see ourselves in a dream
Putting flowers on every table.

Essay on a Blue Field

A blue field came to me and went away
Absorbed by a universe
That knew not what it meant by itself
Only that I should be swallowed
By the field and the blue field swallowed
By its own lovely universe

It does not take much to get intoxicated
Not much at all
We need not a symphony or a rose
Nor a dark feather nor a note
From a lover
We are ever ready to riot and waltz alone
With our own dying forms

But a human might know that nothing
Goes away on a winter morning
That holds a blue field
If the mind is full
And the hive of its plenty
Has not been robbed or sold
If the blue grasses in the wind
Have been held in the shadow of the mime,
The pause at the end of the breath.

The Request

In my short white beard
I am drawing close
To the evening fall of your lips.
I have stopped asking for mercy

Every request I make is without sense
Every request comes from a natural madness
An innocence that has never existed.

The horrible spasms of Rome
Have found their own dark rooms
Without furniture.

A full moon burns in the western clouds
Where were you at 1 a.m.?

A strange unprintable blue
Seeps into the mind of earth
And its dream of the skin

With blood on the pillow
And in the trees.

The Way to You

I knew you at a window and in the coliseum
In the mercury of my stomach.
My hair is still growing at the shore,
My eyes are still blue
And my father is still dead
I awaken cheerful and tolerant.
I know of several small places
That will admit me and remember
Though I have never touched their dusty corners.
The mind wants to hold itself
In the train whistles of my eternity
Where I am still teaching school
In the old brick building by the river.
The mind an abundance of itself
The center of footsteps
On my way to you
Beneath the clouds rising high and deep.

A Word

I want to stare at my martini before I drink it.
To stand atop the snowy hill waiting
Motionless until I am nearly numb
Then walk away toward town as darkness falls.

Each time a word is summoned
It is the miracle of a small storm.
It is a way to breathe, a way to walk.
A fearlessness we can barely understand.

The Uniform

Morning and night
I keep watching the woods at five

A uniform, animated and stuffed
With corn stalks and twisted silverware
Sits at a piano
Or in a white chair beneath a willow   .

It awaits the gift of my rag,
My necktie my stained shoes and shirts
From an old man's closet
It wants my dead brother's coat
That hangs on a hook
Behind my door.

The uniform walks and bends
Into an old song of arms and throats
A crooked row of medals, ribbons
Falling from its chest

Wreathed in pipe smoke, it has taken a seat
Upon a dusty fallen log
Within sight of my bedroom window

Each night in stories for my daughters
I chase it away
Back into the flames of the world.

Water Body

The sea is asleep in a murmur,
The beds unmade in their want
A purpled mania alive in the lost book of gales,
Electric pictures to pass around.
The cells of the wrist
Paint the walls of heaven
With a philosopher's love for the core
That cannot be kissed.

The fruit of the nerve stem
Birthed in a sonnet.
As we sat in the woods
Amid the little piles of snow;
When the deer came close

The light through the tree tops
Needed no blessing nor mending
To place it upon a water body;
All to step back silently
And then away.

Escape from January
> *Who is to say how long a day should be?*
> *–Karen Telford, Autumn 1999*

The face falls into its direction
I want to go everywhere; I go to the sea.

Reading is a way to get lost
As the hands and brain get marked
By veins that few can believe.

Glaciers have passed through our sleep;
Give me back my hair.
So many worlds get closed.

Feet warming in silence,
The radio news indiscernible
My old music teachers
Are probably all dead by now.

If to have no purpose means being open
To all purposes, how many ways
Might a human be welcomed into the world.

In the madness of the jet stream
I have been a good man all day
But it is not enough
The light, the face seemed a fiction
The beautiful objects unreal in their molecules

Hopefully nearby there is someone
Who can play the piano and sing.

The Last Reader on the Beach

The mind turns orange in space
Away from its knowing,
And what remains
Is a white plate of clams.
Then the five sides of a thought
The ascension of a leaf
Stolen from the desert.

How strange to find my father smiling.
He had been just a hand
In a winter scene
Concerning the shadow of my nerves.

Now he has returned to the beach chair
And I have brought him a small meal
On a clean white plate
Lifted from the sea.

The Aztec

Can you find a word for "absence?"
What can I tell you about my losses?
They have already created me several times.

How many times have my limbs returned to me,
Ruined me, saved me…
If I am dried blood I cannot explain it.
If I am silent it is so my shape can be found.

Not far, not close
An animal shadow rises from the ground.
A dark moth comes into my eye
And cannot escape.

When I rode through Mexico
On a bus without you
I thought I might be a dead Aztec
Who brought back the secret
To the man I would become.

The Gaze

The gaze is away and inward
I do not press too hard
Upon the silences of the earth and its parts.
The pasture seems ready to leap
Out of itself and into the sky.

Red wine and high clouds and a mouth waiting
I try not to press too hard,
Twelve words fade in their masks.
Houseflies walking pale windows
Ready for the absent prayer to fill a room.

At the small museum, we loved
The catastrophes upon the wall,
Tender strangers wandering around each other.

No one knows the long grace of the field
I keep all night
Where she waited for me
In the silence of the Portuguese monks
In the dawn of the white sea walls.

O Small Towns of Ohio

Solitary men sit on porches and by windows
In little houses at the edges of fields
Horses get loose and graze
Just outside the windows of large families
Who bring them apples in October
When the fields are tired and dry
And the nights are cool and lost
And rarely formed by a poet or a cop.

Pools of stars clarify the season as they shift
Burning in their ceremonies
On an axis to the yard light.
Someone brings home beer at 6 p.m.
It's time for checkers and astronomical desires
And the dream of white spiders and buckets of rain.

Requiem

I go to the soft prison of the sky
I go away each morning
While the stars burn in their names.
Beyond the angular
Animal steps at dawn
Women weave their lives
Where the field disappears.
A cello is pulled to the edge
Of the late summer bay.
The wind chimes have disappeared
In the ice that is waiting to hold us,
The memory of wild flowers.

Now That We Are Still Thieves

Now that we are still thieves
Our voices release across the sand,
Our mothers allowed to die quietly
And the green field to deepen in dark chatter.

Now that the prison gates are burning
Will you bless me with your tongue
Before sending me off
To make war with the bankers?

Now that the road has completely fractured
Will you forgive my hopeful prediction
Shared over holiday wine?
Let me be a more thorough fool

Praying at the edge of the bed
Above the sea bitten in half
At the nape of the cliff
In the tardy rain.

The field creatures have withdrawn
Into the strange past
That few seem ready to accept
As unreal.

Now that we are still thieves
We have been imprinted
And make our steps
Toward imaginary objects.

The Shrine

In a room of the tropics
A part of his tropical mind
The blood seemed to curl in the vein
He counted his beers
And said another half prayer
Before the distractions returned
And the caravan reappeared
Beyond his northeast window

He kept imagining grass
He believed he could make it grow
Across the mud pit
In the distance, the bright flags of the past
Caught fire and faded

He kept imagining a shrine to the void
That surrounded the room of the tropics
A shrine without weight of form
A glass of wine that disappears
Just before it falls to the floor.

Essay in Late Summer

In that spoken sunlight, the dogs barked
I watched their mouths and felt detached
The moon circled itself in milk
I had to start running
A burning leaf in my mouth
I had to move toward
The crushed shadow of the mountain
The source of all the music in my head
The beginning of all the patience
I would ever find.

An emptiness began to fill with two colors
With light made of water--
And my fear dwindled
To three questions only.
With a murmur of thunder
And a tripling of Vivaldi
Around the pages of a book in late summer
Something had begun
That could not be held
In the corners of one's name
Or upon the shelf of the horizon.

The purple gates opened
And the dogs barked
As I rode my engine of vapor away
And every day a crowd approached a crowd.

The White Lawn Chairs

All cities are distant along with this pencil.
I can still see the street where my father
Is leaving, pulling his blue wagon.
All faces are distant and returning
Especially the milk man
And the boys of Lombardy.

I am living out my life
At the edge of the woods
Unknown and in the middle of everything.
It is a decency to live without demands
And to be foreign under a wide sky
All knowing, always waiting
For the beauty of time to be shaped again,

To continue oneself.
To open one's arms across a world
That has disappeared
With arms that are disappearing,
The white lawn chairs empty
In the un-mowed grass,
One of them tipped on its side,
Another reason to smile
As the children come running
With their bright towels and oranges.

George Eklund is professor emeritus at Morehead State University. His work has appeared in such journals as *The American Poetry Review*, *Beloit Poetry Journal*, *Crazyhorse*, *Epoch*, *The Iowa Review*, *The Massachusetts Review*, *The New Ohio Review*, *The North American Review*, *Rio Grande Review*, *Sycamore Review* and *Willow Springs*.

His publications include the full length collections *The Island Blade* (ABZ Press 2011) and *Each Breath I Cannot Hold* (Wind Publications 2011), and a chapbook from Finishing Line Press in 2012, *Wanting to Be an Element*. He is currently publishing translations of contemporary Latin American poets into English.

www.ingramcontent.com/pod-product-compliance
Lightning Source LLC
LaVergne TN
LVHW041559070426
835507LV00011B/1192